In Dog Years
I'm Dead

In Dog Years I'm Dead

Growing Old (Dis)gracefully

Carol Lynn Pearson

GIBBS SMITH
TO ENRICH AND INSPIRE HUMANKIND

First Edition
16 15 14 13 12   10 9 8 7

Text © 2010 Carol Lynn Pearson

Published by
Gibbs Smith
P.O. Box 667
Layton, Utah 84041

1.800.835.4993 orders
www.gibbs-smith.com

Cover design by Black Eye Design
Interior design by Black Eye Design and Renee Bond
Printed and bound in China
Gibbs Smith books are printed on either recycled, 100% post-
consumer waste, FSC-certified papers or on paper produced
from a 100% certified sustainable forest/controlled wood source.

Library of Congress Cataloging-in-Publication Data

Pearson, Carol Lynn.
  In dog years I'm dead : growing old (dis)gracefully / Carol
Lynn Pearson. — 1st ed.
      p. cm.
  ISBN-13: 978-1-4236-0662-8
  ISBN-10: 1-4236-0662-0
  1. Aging—Humor. I. Title.
  PN6231.A43P43 2010
  818'.5402—dc22
                                    2010009750

You know you're getting older when . . .

SUDDENLY YOU REALIZE . . .

When you do the Hokey Pokey
you put your left hip out—
and it stays out.

You have your choice
of two temptations and
choose the one that will
get you home earlier.

YOU KEEP REPEATING YOURSELF.

You don't care where your spouse goes,

just as long as you
don't have to go along.

You are cautioned
to slow down
by the doctor
instead of by the police.

You're sitting in a rocker and
can't get it started.

You keep repeating yourself.

"Getting a little action"

means you don't need
to take any fiber today.

"Getting lucky"
means you find your car
in the parking lot.

An **"all-nighter"**
means you didn't have to get up to pee.

You choose cereal
for the fiber, not the toy.

You stoop to tie your shoes and wonder what else you can do while you're down there.

You learn never to
take a sleeping pill
and a laxative
on the same night.

Your back
goes out more than you do.

Your sweetie says,
"Let's go upstairs and make love,"
and you answer,
"Pick one, I can't do both!"

YOU KEEP REPEATING YOURSELF.

You wonder how you got

over the hill

without getting to the top.

You're sitting on a park bench, and a Boy Scout comes up and helps you cross your legs.

You realize that dates on the calendar are **closer** than they appear.

You know it all;
you just can't remember it all at once!

You look

← **BOTH WAYS** →

before crossing a room.

You find that you're big into
swing dancing,
though not on purpose.

Some parts of your body

are just prone to swinging.

You spend a lot of time thinking about the hereafter—walking into the next room and saying, "What in the world am I here after?"

You decide
that if God
wanted you to
touch your toes,
he would have
put them on
your knees.

You don't just jump into things anymore. In fact, you don't jump at all.

You Keep On Hand
Medications Like...

BUYAGRA

Injectable stimulant taken prior to shopping.
Increases potency and duration of spending spree.

EMPTY NESTROGEN

Highly effective suppository that eliminates
melancholy by enhancing the memory of how awful
your kids were as teenagers and how you couldn't
wait until they moved out.

DAMITOL

Take two and the rest of the world can go to hell
for up to 8 hours.

Your Personal Hit Parade Includes These Artists and Their Great Tunes:

The Bee Gees–"How Can You Mend a Broken Hip?"

Herman's Hermits–"Mrs. Brown, You've Got a Lovely Walker"

Marvin Gaye–"I Heard It Through the Grape Nuts"

Procol Harum–"A Whiter Shade of Hair"

Johnny Nash–"I Can't See Clearly Now"

Leo Sayer–"You Make Me Feel Like Nappin'"

ABBA–"Denture Queen"

Paul Simon–"Fifty Ways to Lose Your Liver"

Carly Simon—"You're So Varicose Vein"

Roberta Flack—"The First Time Ever I Forgot Your Face"

Commodores—"Once, Twice, Three Times to the Bathroom"

Rolling Stones—"You Can't Always Pee When You Want"

Bobby Darin—"Splish, Splash, I Was Havin' a Flash"

Nancy Sinatra—"These Boots Were Made for Bunions"

The Who—"Talkin' 'Bout My Medication"

The Beatles—"I Get By with a Little Help from Depends"

Three sisters—ages 92, 94 and 96—live in a house together.

One night the 96-year-old draws a bath. She puts her foot in and pauses. She yells to the other sisters, "Was I getting in or out of the bath?"

The 94-year-old yells back, "I don't know. I'll come up and see." She starts up the stairs and pauses. "Was I going up the stairs or down?"

The 92-year-old is sitting at the kitchen table listening to her sisters. She shakes her head and says, "I sure hope I never get that forgetful." She knocks on wood for good measure. She then yells, "I'll come up and help both of you as soon as I see who's at the door."

YOU FIND THAT
REMINISCING ISN'T
WHAT IT USED TO BE,

BUT STILL . . .

Then—

you were into acid rock.

Now—

you're into acid reflux.

Then—

you thought about moving to
California because it's cool.

Now—

you think about moving to
California because it's warm.

Then—
you were growing pot.

Now—
you're growing a potbelly.

Then—

you were popping pills, smoking joints.

Now—

you're popping joints.

Then—

you were getting out to a hip new joint.

Now—

you're getting a new hip joint.

Then—
you were big on the Rolling Stones.

Now—
you're big on kidney stones.

Then—
you took acid.

Now—
you take antacid.

Then—
you were hoping for a BMW.

Now—
you are hoping for a BM.

Two elderly women were out driving in a large car—both could barely see over the dashboard. As they were cruising along they came to an intersection. The stoplight was red but they just went on through.

The woman in the passenger seat thought to herself, "I must be losing it. I could have sworn we just went through a red light."

After a few more minutes they came to another intersection and the light was red again, and again they went right through. This time the woman in the passenger seat was almost sure that the light had been red but was really concerned that she was losing it. She was getting nervous and decided to pay very close attention to the road and the next intersection to see what was going on.

At the next intersection, sure enough, the light was definitely red and they went right through. She turned to the other woman and said, "Dorothy! Did you know you just ran through three red lights in a row! You could have killed us!"

Dorothy turned to her and said, "Oh, am I driving?"

Mildred was a 93-year-old woman who was particularly despondent over the recent death of her husband Earl. She decided that she would just kill herself and join him in death.

Thinking that it would be best to get it over with quickly, she took out Earl's old army pistol and made the decision to shoot herself in the heart since it was so badly broken in the first place. Not wanting to miss this vital organ and become a vegetable and a burden to someone, she called her doctor's office to inquire as to just exactly where the heart would be. "Your heart would be just below your left breast," the doctor said.

Later that night, Mildred was admitted to the hospital with a bullet wound to her left knee.

IF YOU HAPPEN TO BE FEMALE . . .

You go in for a mammogram
and realize this is
your last chance
to appear topless in film.

You stand naked
in front of a mirror and can
see your rear end
without turning around.

The growth of hair on your legs slows down, giving you **plenty of time** to care for your newly acquired mustache.

You no longer have upper arms;
you have wingspans!

You realize that
of all the curves
life has thrown you,
you're sitting on
the biggest one.

Your memory starts to go
and the one thing you can retain is
water.

Going braless
pulls all the wrinkles out of your face.

You begin to ponder the Big Questions: What is life? Why am I here? How much Healthy Choice ice cream can I eat before it's no longer a healthy choice?

Your workout philosophy becomes
"no pain, no pain."

Come to think of it,
you're already in shape–
round is a shape!

You finally know what
Victoria's Secret is:

*nobody older than thirty
can fit into her stuff.*

YOUR PERSONAL AD READS . . .

Foxy Lady: Sexy, blue-haired beauty, slim, 5'4" (used to be 5'6"), many new parts, including hip, knee, cornea, valves. Doesn't run, but walks well.

OR:

Mint Condition Male: High mileage, some hair. If you're a groovy chick or a swinging hen, let's get together to listen to my boss collection of eight-track tapes.

You ask your sweetie . . .
Whatever happened to
our sexual relations?

And you hear . . .
I don't know. I don't think we
even got a Christmas card
from them this year.

Diana reached her sixty-fifth birthday and prayed, "Dear Lord, this life is so great. Please, please let me live until I'm a hundred!"

The Lord replied, "My dear, your prayer is granted."

Well, Diana was so excited that she went to the plastic surgeon and had some work done on her eyes, her chin, her boobs, her tummy. Then she went to the hairdresser and got a brand new color and style, and then to her favorite store for an entire new wardrobe. Thrilled, she stepped out onto the curb just in time to be run over by a Mack truck.

Opening her eyes in heaven, she said, "Wait, wait! Lord—you promised me I could live until I was a hundred!"

The Lord looked at her and said, "Oh! I'm sorry, my dear. I didn't *recognize* you!"

YOU FIND YOURSELF PLAYING FUN GAMES LIKE . . .

Hide and Go Pee

Twenty Questions
   shouted into your good ear

Kick the Bucket

Red Rover, Red Rover,
   the Nurse says Bend Over

Musical Recliners

Simon Says Something Incoherent

Haven't got a Clue

Flabble

Lost Your Marbles

Sag, You're It

Pin the Toupee on the Bald Guy

Spin the Bottle of Mylanta

The Senility Prayer

Grant me the senility to forget the people I never liked anyway, the good fortune to run into the ones I do, and the eyesight to tell the difference.

YOU FINALLY UNDERSTAND THE NATURE OF SUCCESS

At age 4 success is ... not peeing in your pants.

At 12 success is ... having friends.

At 16 success is ... having a driver's license.

At 20 success is ... having sex.

At 35 success is ... having money.

At 50 success is ... having money.

At 60 success is ... having sex.

At 70 success is ... having a driver's license.

At 75 success is ... having friends.

At 80 success is ... not peeing in your pants.

I feel like my body has gotten totally out of shape, so I got my doctor's permission to join a fitness club and start exercising. I decided to take an aerobics class for seniors. I bent, twisted, gyrated, jumped up and down, and perspired for an hour. By the time I got my leotards on, the class was over.

YOU LOOK FORWARD TO GETTING EVEN OLDER BECAUSE . . .

At 104 there's no peer pressure.

You finally realize you can't take life seriously. Nobody **gets out alive** anyway.

You can let housework go.

Occasionally say, "Dust? But this is where Mother wanted us to scatter her ashes."

You can still enjoy an active, passionate sex life—provided you get cable or that dish thing.

You know that birthdays are nature's way of telling us to **EAT MORE CAKE.**

You can forget about taking walks. Aunt Mabel started walking five miles a day when she was 60. She's 97 now and nobody has any idea where she is.

You like to be **in crowds** because they keep you from falling down.

You get to hear
"snap, crackle, pop"
before you get to breakfast.

You know your secrets are safe with your friends

because they can't
remember them either.

Fewer and fewer things seem worth waiting in line for.

THREE GOOD THINGS ABOUT GETTING SENILE ARE, YOU GET TO . . .

1. Meet new people every day.
2. Hide your own Easter eggs.
3. Meet new people every day.

Jacob, age 92, and Rebecca, age 89, are all excited about their decision to get married. They go for a stroll to discuss the wedding and on the way they pass a drugstore. Jacob suggests they go in.

"Are you the owner?" Jacob asks the pharmacist.

"Yes," says the pharmacist.

Says Jacob: "We're about to get married. Do you sell heart medication?"

Pharmacist: "Of course we do."

Jacob: "How about medicine for circulation?"

Pharmacist: "All kinds."

Jacob: "Medicine for rheumatism?"

Pharmacist: "Definitely."

Jacob: "How about Viagra?"

Pharmacist: "Of course."

Jacob: "Medicine for memory problems, arthritis, jaundice?"

Pharmacist: "Yes, a large variety. The works."

Jacob: "What about vitamins, sleeping pills, Geritol, antidotes for Parkinson's disease?"

Pharmacist: "Absolutely."

Jacob: "You sell wheelchairs and walkers?"

Pharmacist: "All speeds and sizes."

Finally Jacob says to the pharmacist: "We'd like to register here for our wedding gifts, please."

"The most unfair thing about life is the way it ends. I mean, life is tough. It takes up a lot of your time. What do you get at the end of it? A Death! What's that, a bonus? I think the life cycle is all backwards. You should die first, get it out of the way. Then you live in an old age home. You get kicked out when you're too young, you get a gold watch, you go to work. You work forty years until you're young enough to enjoy your retirement. You do drugs, alcohol, you party, you get ready for high school. You go to grade school, you become a kid, you play, you have no responsibilities, you become a little baby, you go back into the womb, you spend your last nine months floating . . .

. . . and you finish off as an orgasm."

—**George Carlin**

You Answer Ads Like...

FOR SALE: antique desk suitable for lady with thick legs and large drawers.

There is more money being spent on breast implants and Viagra than on Alzheimer's research. This means that by 2020, there should be a large elderly population with perky appendages and absolutely no recollection of what to do with them.

YOU HEAR YOUR
FRIENDS SAY (IF THEY
SHOUT LOUD ENOUGH)
THINGS LIKE . . .

My memory's not as sharp as it used to be.

Also, my memory's not as sharp as it used to be.

Now that food has replaced sex in my life, I can't even get into **my own pants.**

I started out with nothing . . . I still have most of it.

When did my **wild oats** turn to prunes and All-Bran?

Funny, I don't remember being **absentminded.**

I finally got
all of my stuff together
and now I can't remember
where I put it.

Whisky really does improve with age.

The older I get, the more I like it.

I wonder if
buying green bananas is such a
good investment.

The other day, I was reading about how our aging population is growing, and in the same magazine, a medical report explained how we shrink with age. What's this? My age group is growing and shrinking at the same time?

At my age, happy hour is nap time.

I don't let aging get me down—
it's too hard to
get back up!

I don't worry about
avoiding temptation anymore.
It avoids me!

I don't do drugs.
At my age
I get the same effect
just standing up fast.

I still have something on the ball. I'm just too tired to bounce it.

I've only got one other speed and **it's slower.**

When I was young
we used to go "skinny-dipping."
Now I just "chunky-dunk."

Brain cells come and brain cells go, but **fat cells** live forever.

Lying about my age

is easier now that
I often forget what it is.

In dog years, I'm dead!

You *BECOME* 21.
You *TURN* 30.
You're *PUSHING* 40.
You *REACH* 50.
You *MAKE IT* to 60.
Then you build up so much speed you *HIT* 70!
After that, it's a day-by-day thing.

—**excerpted from George Carlin**

These days about half the
stuff in my shopping cart says
"For fast relief."

You find it's time to learn the senior dress code...

THE FOLLOWING COMBINATIONS DO NOT GO TOGETHER AND SHOULD BE AVOIDED.

- A nose ring and bifocals
- Spiked hair and bald spots
- A pierced tongue and dentures
- Miniskirts and support hose
- Ankle bracelets and corn pads

- Speedos and cellulite
- A belly button ring and a gall bladder surgery scar
- Unbuttoned disco shirts and a heart monitor
- Midriff shirts and a midriff bulge
- Bikinis and liver spots
- Short shorts and varicose veins
- In-line skates and a walker
- Thongs and Depends

A couple had been married for 40 years and also celebrated their 60th birthdays.

During the celebration, a fairy appeared and said that because they had been such a loving couple all these years, she would give them one wish each.

Being the faithful, loving spouse for all these years, naturally the wife wanted for herself and her husband to have a romantic vacation together, so she wished for them to travel around the world.

The fairy waved her wand and boom! The wife had the tickets in her hand.

Next, it was the husband's turn and the fairy assured him he could have any wish he wanted, all he needed to do was ask for his heart's desire.

He paused for a moment and then said, "Well, honestly, I'd like to have a woman 30 years younger than me."

The fairy picked up her wand and kazoom! The husband turned 90!

YOU AGREE WITH
THOSE WHO MANAGED
TO GET BOTH OLD AND
FAMOUS THAT . . .

The secret of
staying young
is to live honestly,
eat slowly, and
lie about your age.

—**Lucille Ball**

OLD AGE: First you forget names, then you forget faces, then you forget to pull your zipper up, then you forget to pull your zipper down.

—**Leo Rosenberg**

When men reach their sixties and retire
they go to pieces.
Women just go right on cooking.

—**Gail Sheehy**

True terror is to wake up one morning
and discover that
your high school class
is running the country.

—**Kurt Vonnegut**

You can live to be a hundred
if you give up
all the things that make you
want to live to be a hundred.

—**Woody Allen**

I intend to live forever,
or die trying.

—**Groucho Marx**

Oh, to be seventy again!

—Oliver Wendell Holmes,
on seeing an attractive lady at his 95th birthday

If you live to be one hundred,
YOU'VE GOT IT MADE.
Very few people die past that age.

—**George Burns**

You know you're getting old when everything hurts. And what doesn't hurt **doesn't work.**

—**Hy Gardner**

I'M SO OLD THEY'VE CANCELLED MY BLOOD TYPE.

—Bob Hope

Nice to be here?
At my age it's nice to be
anywhere.

—**George Burns**

AND YOU'RE ESPECIALLY GRATEFUL THAT WHEN ALL IS SAID AND DONE . . .

In the end, it's not the
years in your life that count.
It's the life in your years.

—**Abraham Lincoln**

It's not how old you are,
but how you are old.

—**Marie Dressler**

When Grandma Moses's arthritis made manipulating a needle too difficult, she turned from sewing to painting. She created 2,000 paintings after the age of seventy.

To keep the
HEART UNWRINKLED,
to be hopeful, kindly, cheerful,
reverent—that is
to triumph over old age.

—**Thomas B. Aldrich**

Remember:

You don't stop laughing because you grow old. You grow old because you stop laughing.

—Michael Pritchard

AS WE GROW OLD . . .
THE BEAUTY STEALS INWARD.

—**Ralph Waldo Emerson**

Beautiful young people are
accidents of nature,
but beautiful old people are
works of art.

—**Eleanor Roosevelt**

The great thing about getting older is that you don't lose all the other ages you've been.

—**Madeleine L'Engle**

Do these Depends make my butt look big?